IT TAKES A VILLAGE

IT
TAKES
A
VILLAGE

SPINNING THE
COLLECTIVE YARN

THE 2023 PRATT LECTURE

PETER BALKWILL

BREAKWATER
P.O. Box 2188, St. John's, NL, Canada, A1C 6E6
www.breakwaterbooks.com

COPYRIGHT © 2023 Peter Balkwill
ISBN 978-1-55081-965-6
Back cover buffalo puppet image: Mike Tan Photo
A CIP catalogue record for this book is available from
Library and Archives Canada.

The main typeface used throughout this book is Adobe
Jenson Pro. Adobe Jenson Pro captures the essence of
Nicolas Jenson's roman and Ludovico degli Arrighi's italic
typeface designs. The combined strength and beauty of these
two icons of Renaissance type result in an elegant typeface
suited to a broad spectrum of applications. Designed by
Robert Slimbach, Adobe Jenson Pro provides a power and
flexibility for text composition rarely found in digital type.

We acknowledge the support of the Canada Council for the
Arts. We acknowledge the financial support of the Government
of Canada and the Government of Newfoundland and
Labrador through the Department of Tourism, Culture,
Arts and Recreation for our publishing activities.

PRINTED AND BOUND IN CANADA.

Breakwater Books is committed to choosing papers and
materials for our books that help to protect our environment.
To this end, this book is printed on recycled paper that is
certified by the Forest Stewardship Council®.

I dedicate this lecture to my parents,
who managed to raise an artist,
and to my family—Nan, Walker, and Juno—
who continue to raise me as an artist.
It is a remarkable journey.

THE scene is an empty stage with a podium and microphone. There is a side table with a small plastic bottle of water. The centre dwellings of the stage are lit with a pronounced spot. The lecture is set to start . . . Five minutes go past the posted start time before the HOST comes out to settle the gathered public. A general introduction is delivered, including a short, formal bio.

The HOST then looks off and up to stage right. There is an awkward pause. Something must be wrong. The HOST begins to go back up stage right. The stage is bare for a moment. The HOST returns looking bewildered but maintaining a sense of decorum. They stand at the podium for a moment with their concern focused up and off stage right.

A slight bustle up stage left. OUR HERO enters dragging a long, seemingly unending piece of paper, while also balancing several sheets of loose-leaf, a reusable bottle of water, and a small, old, tattered suitcase. As he enters, the HOST encourages a round of applause from the gathered public.

OUR HERO makes it to centre stage. He juggles his luggage and bric-a-brac to formally shake the hand of the HOST and goes on in an awkward way to settle his belongings. There is a short moment between the two where neither knows where to go next. Then OUR HERO hugs the HOST, which goes on a little longer than normal. He turns to address the gathered public.

Lectio Praecursoria:

Learned colleagues, faculty of the Department of English, organizers of the Pratt Lecture, students, people of St. John's. Hallowed Longshoremen . . . Longshorepeople . . . Folks . . . Longshorefolks.

My thanks for this occasion and taking time out of your busy lives to attend, to gather, to speak upon the nature of Story. I apologize for my lateness. (*He looks upstage from his entrance.*) I was . . . there was a . . . uhhh . . . it's a long story.

Nonetheless . . . here we are.

He settles.

Thomas King, the well-known Indigenous writer and broadcast presenter, suggests that the "truth about stories is that that's all we are." He says: "You cannot understand the world without telling a story."[1] I know he suggests this because he made a gift of these words to a recent project I was part of called *Iniskim: Return of the Buffalo*, an immersive puppet-lantern performance that celebrates the reintegration of bison into the natural environment.

Interesting story about the bison: there were once over three hundred million that roamed the mixed prairie grasslands. Their numbers were so vast and they moved in such concert with each other and the environment that to see them must have been like witnessing some kind of giant meat glacier slowly rumbling across the land. A massive forest of hair inching and grunting in harmony in the environment—remarkable.

As the story goes—as the story I was given to understand the world by goes—they were hunted by overzealous settlers who were beguiled by the profits they could gain from

---

[1] First Rider, Amethyst, et al. *Iniskim: Return of the Buffalo*. Canadian Academy of Mask and Puppetry Archives, 2022. Script.

the fur industry, not even for the value of their meat and bones. Or else they were hunted by tourists from Europe who just wanted to shoot one so they would have that story to tell back in fancy parlours over caviar and vodka. There were other people, the people of First Nations, who were living and hunting these animals as well, folks who had been around for as long as the animals themselves. These people managed to live in balance with these creatures, using them to provide not only a way of life, using every bit of the animal to survive, but also imbedding themselves and the animal into a story of life that goes deeper than many of us can fathom.

In the mid-1800s, the American government, in the interests of "progress" and of trans-continental expansion, discovered that they couldn't suppress many of the Indigenous people who had already done the business of establishing a nation here. They were having particular trouble with the Sioux Nation. The army decided to use subversive military tactics and went after the food source: they killed the buffalo. The Canadian government, forming at the time and having similar troubles with Indigenous dwellers, issued the same proclamation. Kill the buffalo. The operative word, spanning the story I was told as a kid and the one I later discovered, is "hunt" or "exterminate."

That is a tragic story. At least, that part of the story is tragic—but it is only one chapter of a larger story. I started telling it as a good story, a story that even carries the words "celebration," and "environment," and—"puppet."

It's true: under "occupation," my passport states "puppeteer." My brother is annoyed at this and tells me I should get that changed because it will only create troubles at the border and result in higher levels of having to go into the back room for secondary inspections. The last time we drove to the States his wish came true—for both of us.

I believe that a truth about puppets is that they come to you: the puppet chooses the puppeteer. The first puppet that ever found me was in the basement of my best friend's house. It was a hinged-jaw puppet. "Hinged jaw" means that its mouth could move, so it looked like it was talking when I moved it. It was a Franciscan monk, and it had the Franciscan monk hair thing, a tonsure, and it was dressed in a brown robe and it was called Algernon. I picked it up and it just started talking and it made everyone laugh, uttering unspeakably rude things. The parents of my friend said, "You should take that home; we have no idea where it came from and our children never play with it." Twenty-five years later I found myself among a group of friends who also decided to put the word "puppeteer" under "occupation" on their passports:

Justin (Judd) Palmer
Steve (Pityu) Kenderes
Robert (Bobby) Hall
Steve (Pearce) Pearce

As this story goes, we all met working as staff at a summer camp in the Rocky Mountains. Our summer days were filled with backcountry adventures and the complete abandonment of all things connected to adult responsibility. As maturing men, we thrived in this environment. The intensity of it was akin to the chapter of life that I'd just completed: serving four years in the United States Navy. Summer camp is a place where story thrives, because we are all sequestered from the norms of daily life. Strange folks living with strangers in a strange situation, sleeping in strange bunks where fire gives comfort in the face of the dark, devious world around us. People are vulnerable here, open to needing each other, open to the collective sense-making of this place, open to Making

Story so as to understand this experience. Being pulled out of the comforts of routine fuelled the thrill of learning about creatures like the Goat-Man, half-goat and half-man, who wears a hook for a hand and consumes wayward souls that stray from the safety of the group. In fact, he lives just over there, in a dilapidated cabin, and if we're all game we can sneak out past midnight under the light of the full moon and witness his ritual of cannibalistic fury. No one ever did witness it, but to make sure that the story bamboozled even the heartiest summer-camp skeptic, footprints were crafted to indicate that something had spied on us as we slept. No doubt there were countless phone calls at the end of summer from concerned parents who'd been told by their children that their counsellors were devil-worshippers. We decided to make a pact to live our lives this way—forever. Our way of fulfilling that pact was to form a puppet company and call it the Old Trout Puppet Workshop.

We built our first show in residence on a ranch in southern Alberta, in exchange for doing various farm chores: collecting and washing the eggs, feeding the livestock, being extra careful of the pigs. The pigs. "The pigs: they'll fucking kill ya, man," as Pityu muttered in the throes of some fitful dream before we headed back to the farm.[2] We decided that it was best to leave the goats alone, because those square pupils are just a little too close to the Underworld. There was a great turkey epidemic that landed just before Thanksgiving that year and we had to put the herd—flock?—herd of turkey down. The birds, infected by some rampant avian flu, had to be euthanized and burnt en masse to prevent the sickness from spreading to other livestock. This was an onerous task, culminating in an enormous pyre that we had to tend, due to fire hazards. The whole event caused a level of trauma that likely went into our first show. We're still working through it today.

For doing all these things, our landlords, the ranchers, gave us free rent and a workshop in which to make puppets, and wood, and tools. And all the meat we could eat. Our first show was called *The Unlikely Birth of Istvan* and we premiered it in the bunkhouse to a group of Mennonite cowboys and Hutterites— possibly the best audience we have ever had. *Istvan* would go on to be performed here, at the LSPU Hall in St. John's, as part of Festival Five. There was a singing pig and it was murdered. Perhaps a fitting artistic revenge for

2 Kenderes, Pityu. *Some Fitful Dream: Its Throes*. Slumberland Press, 1999.

haunting Pityu's nightmares. Blood sprayed all over the set. That scene almost caused riots on Jellybean Row.

And so there were five of us who decided to give it a go, making stories with puppets. We were seemingly simple creatures, but with deep complexities. We liked our hair to grow shaggy and our beards to grow scraggly and we preferred to wear grubby, unchanged denim and plaid shirts with layers of dust imbedded from days of carving, and we were oblivious to the fact that as a carcinogen, wood dust sits at Number Three, whereas cigarettes land at Number Seven on the mythical list of what to avoid when you want to live a long and healthy life. But how are you supposed to wear a dust mask with a smoke in your mouth? We moved about the studio communicating in meaning-full grunts, preparing ourselves for our task of hunting ways to create visual story. There was something early-humanish about us, we thought; we worked "from the prehistoric part of our hearts, that part which trembles in the face of the cold crags and the hoar-blasted prairie, and knows what the Neanderthal knew: that the lone straggler is lost."[3]

---

[3] Palmer, Judd. "To Be Honest, We Devised Theatre Companies Are Kind of like Gangs." *Canadian Theatre Review*, vol. 135, Summer 2008, pp. 17-20.

It could be argued that puppetry is among our earliest forms of storytelling. The puppet is only a thing that is a representation of another thing. In the dank caves of old, we would gather together and use bits of fur and string to bind together rocks and sticks and make this whole, rough assemblage resemble that ... thing ... that thing half-goat half-man out there in the dangerous world, and we would use these haphazard dolls to fumblingly relate the story of how poor Gog was trampled for getting too close to its giant hoof-foot. We didn't have a name for the creature inspiring the story so we created effigies of it and danced it around, animating it, and we would grunt together until our expressions found commonality, and out of this tentative and faltering group work a word emerged.

He demonstrates with low, guttural grunts.

"Groaattmun ... Geaoutmum ... Goat-Man."

At least this is how I like to imagine that we developed skills in our telling of things, and who's to really know? A great enabler, our imagination, useful in so many ways.

There is something deeply gratifying about going into antique shops. They are museums where you are allowed to pick up and actually hold the object of interest. And I have something of an obsessive collecting disorder born out of my fascination with old things previously owned and dusted with the sediment of story. Puppeteers tend to be hoarders. I've never seen a puppeteer's studio that wasn't festooned with endless boxes of stuff all placed in dangerous stacks for want of being able to throw anything out. The actual name of my company should be the Old Trout Precariously Placed Bins of Shit Workshop. I have a friend who likes to acquire things out of antique shops and then tell his kids stories of how they used to belong to some distant ancestor. This friend has the most interesting lineage of anyone I know, his own life raised to the rank of remarkable . . . and true because he imagines it to be so.

It may be true that story is like breath and in the same way that we need to be always breathing air, so too must we always be with story. It is a vital part of our physical being. We absorb story into our body through something akin to osmosis, add to it, and send it back out into the world, altered in a way that connects us to all life in the cosmos. This is the cycle of our yarn, and it's difficult to articulate the origin of its journey—in fact this is the basis for many of life's greatest conflicts. Nonetheless, stories move through us in such a way that we pass them on to others. Historically, the only way to do this was through a direct interaction with each other that required some form of physical proximity, to speak the words, or to read them upon pages of paper on which the text had been written in ink by hand. This process required an investment of time that allowed us to live with the story and to make sense of it before exhaling it back out and into humanity. Through digital means, we now have so many more ways to share them that we are exceeding our ability to live at length with individual, singular story, and the material does not have the time to become absorbed into our cellular structure. Tossed upon unseen currents, we flit from one to the next without ever immersing ourselves in the content.

I heard an article on CBC a while back, lingering to catch the words as I bounced around different radio stations while driving the car; I couldn't even begin to remember what the program was, but it was suggesting that our mounting mental health crisis is in some way linked to the fact that we don't work as much with our hands as we used to. That a hundred years ago—even fifty years ago—we sustained ourselves through daily physical acts: chopping wood for the fire, picking vegetables from a garden that we'd planted ourselves, fixing our socks because they had a hole in them—simple things like this. Reflecting on this idea, I recalled how much I valued working in the costume shop for the production hours of my theatre-training program. While stitching the fabric into clothing, I felt a sense of peace, as though I was underwater, and the stories flowed easily from those around me also working. They landed in such intimate and personal ways. I suddenly understood the point of Quilting Bees. The digital age is changing that, and in the great convenience of things we are slowly evolving away from humanity as we know it toward a great unknown, and yet all of it still driven by our insatiable need for story.

Perhaps the holistic experience is one of the reasons I find assurance in the art of puppetry. It must be that . . . or maybe the rampant fame that comes through the practice. It's true the celebrity is extraordinary, but I like to think it's the former. Puppetry is an analogue form of storytelling. One answer to "Why do we find puppetry performance so compelling?" is "Because it takes us backwards instead of forwards." In an age where every billboard tells you how and why you need to keep pace with our changing world, puppetry pulls us back to a simpler existence. We are creatures prone to the malady of nostalgia, after all; inside all of us there is a small wonder about the possibility of past lives. Some distant connection to an ancestor that lived eight, ten, twenty generations ago (perhaps why I don't mind the grate of bagpipes). In a manner of speaking we are all of us connected in a cellular way to our mothers and grandmothers even before we are born. A woman who holds a daughter in utero holds that daughter's eggs developing within her, too. Like the passage of warmth through objects touching, perhaps our innate way of being is to connect back in a manner that makes sense for our bodies more than our minds. To not be charging headfirst into the next level of technological wizardry.

To create a puppet show you must first build the puppets. Well, first, actually, you choose the story you want to share, or the story you think you want to share, for something happens when you start to build the puppets that will become the characters in this tale— the puppets themselves change the direction of things. You build them with specific tasks in mind that will serve the plot of your story, but once you start to play with them, they demonstrate things that they do with great efficiency . . . things you didn't expect . . . and so you change the story to fit this action, which has its own effect upon the arc of the plot, begging for new puppets to be added, which will in turn have their own impact on things. You suddenly discover yourself collaborating with an unknown force in the universe, as if the cosmos itself was your dramaturge. It's an exciting phenomenon.

Here you are working with your hands, sharing your deepest thoughts through story with your puppet cohort in the Crafting Bee, as it were, building the objects that lurch into the grand visual poem that will be your show, and you discover a very grounded sense of being with story and with others. Our work in the Trout studio sits in a familial tradition. That is to say that we invest in the human need to rely on others, to count on them to hold your back through the perils of art-making—to love each other beyond all other ambitions. As we work in our studio, we carry a tradition that resembles certain other philosophies, that of the Quakers, for instance, who hold that you ascend to the heavens through a rigid dedication and attention to detail in working with (carving) wood. Because we care about one another, we are able to push ourselves as deep as possible into the art. We call it bare-knuckled creation. And we are there for one another to offer comfort and support when the art punches back and pummels us against the ropes of failure and inadequacy.

These are the qualities that allow us as an ensemble to discover our creative process as a collaborative one. It takes us back to those extended backcountry sojourns we made as camp counsellors. Back when we needed to get a team of ten strangers to work in perfect unison, embracing every menial task as though it were the most important, just to survive the perils of nature. If you want to make a strong ensemble, take them for five days off-trail into the Rocky Mountains, where the bears sleep, and the snow falls suddenly, and the porcupine fucks with grunting ferocity. You'll discover the true sense of needing each other.

I've heard it said that it's impossible to truly collaborate in the creative process. According to this argument, someone needs to be suggesting the singular way forward and the group needs to consent to this singular way—ergo you always have a leader with the group following, even if the place of that leader changes or is passed around. I think this argument comes from someone who hasn't fully found their ensemble. Some folks suggest that it is a rare thing for an artistic group to discover itself, an anomaly, for at the outset each person needs to forsake their singular identity for the sake of the collective, and this is a difficult proposition to the emerging artist who is bent on defining themselves within a competitive industry. And then there is the challenge of time and gained experience.

Our first collaboration as the Old Trouts was our most successful because we'd never done it before and none of us knew what we were doing. We were a silo of bumpkins all asking questions as opposed to knowing answers. We needed each other. Bumpkin to bumpkin trying to do this thing, alongside the unassuming task of farm chores to earn our rent—something else that none of us had ever dealt with before, a perfectly comple- menting unassociated assignment. As we worked on our show we would find ourselves sitting in circles with the unsolvable questions between us, poking them with different ideas and always surprised by how the answers formed themselves. The result was something none of us could have predicted. It happened and we all took a step forward.

In our next project this collaborative process deteriorated just a little bit because each of us had learnt something in the previous journey that we felt was important to investigate further. "A little learning is a dangerous thing"—because it beguiles you into thinking that your perception of things is reality. Now we all wanted to ply our art from our experience. Perhaps this is where the true nature of our bumpkin-ness saved us, because under our thickening skin lived that fragile ego that at the end of the day needed the friend more than the glory of the accomplished artist. An interesting template has been applied to the lifespan of bands, and if you look at collective theatre-creation companies, they are very similar. Bands usually last about two to three years and then they fall apart for various reasons but mostly because the members have developed strong and differing opinions on how they should move forward. If they make it past this, the next hurdle is at the seven-year mark, then at the ten-, then at the twenty-, and past that it is likely for life, probably because they've forfeited the ability to do or define themselves in any other way and are now bound to the end. A notion of having gone all in, fully investing in their bluff against fate. (*He smiles a great, beaming, terrified smile out to the audience.*) This is what my poker face looks like. (*He recaptures his confident façade.*) Predicting the longevity of creation companies is far from an exact science, but to me this template makes sense.

The Old Trouts have extended past Year 23, even, and we still look for that harmony in collaboration, that perfect marriage of ingredients that will produce a simple loaf of freshly baked bread—something to survive on. You can never really articulate the true recipe but rather constantly pursue it like some kind of culinary Holy Grail. And we continue to invest in the puppet. That curious inanimate object, then, may be the butter and garlic to the meal, that thing binding us all together, for it's an agent that can't live without collaboration.

If we look closely at the equation of story relayed in conventional theatre, we see a conflict of egos in play—those of the audience and the actor. An actor walks onstage, assuming the character of Hamlet. The audience members must suspend disbelief and invest in this impersonation as a reality; at least, that is the hope of the artists. There is a moment, however fleeting, that occurs when the audience members must grapple with their ego's consent to the ego of the actor who is presuming to accomplish an impossible task: to become someone else before our very eyes. Let's say that in many cases, as a result of a rigorous rehearsal process and years of training and practice, the actor succeeds. But in this manner the ego of the audience has only been assuaged into accepting the proposition that we are witnessing the character.

In the case of puppetry, we are asking of the performer nothing less than this: we are asking the performer to create a frog out of a block of wood. But the block of wood that will become the puppet does not have an ego; it begs for one. The puppeteer begins to practise the charity and extends their ego to the puppet, but this is only enough to make the puppet move in the manner of the frog and to engage in the moment with an intention connected to the dramatic tension on stage. More is needed. The audience's ego is now called upon to finish the moment: it's their participation that's required to make the frog live. Other puppeteers might argue that this formula I've put before you isn't quite accurate—we all have our fancy ways to sound intelligent—but most puppeteers will agree that any attempted explanation is inadequate, and that the process is always ultimately inexplicable, so for the time being we can propose this possibility, among many others. When puppetry works, there is something of an out-of-body experience that occurs for both the puppeteer and the observer, and it could be suggested that this is a result of actually projecting ourselves into this distant object. We feel the request for assistance, and since each of us has within us our own strongest ego, we rise to the challenge. The result is almost alchemical, and for just the right amount of time the collective gathering conjures an actual frog upon the stage. True collaboration in story-making. This phenomenon could be expressed in another way as well, which would tie it to the foundation of a large part of my training.

In my conservatory theatre training I engaged in three years of vigorous physical work tied to the modalities of Tadashi Suzuki. Prior to this training I studied Ki aikido, which is also a Japanese practice and is tied to many of the foundations of Mr. Suzuki's principles of building ensemble:

> Extend your Ki (or, in the case of Suzuki's work, the energy tied to your inner sensibilities).
> Know your partner's mind (in this case, that of your audience and co-performers).
> Respect your partner's Ki.
> Put yourself in your partner's place.
> Lead with confidence.

Professors Steve Pearson and Robyn Hunt, the directors of my conservatory program at the University of Washington in Seattle, were among Mr. Suzuki's early tenured Western theatre practitioners back in the early '80s. Pearson had also trained in aikido with Master B. J. Carlisle in San Diego, California, and he tirelessly investigated Ki in all things concerned with live performance. It is fair to suggest that most arts within Japanese culture are associated with the practice of Ki. Without forethought I'd prepared myself perfectly for this union.

I can recall sitting in painful positions in aikido class prior to my actor training, listening to my sensei at the Calgary Ki Society as he spoke endlessly about the nature of Ki and calm water reflecting the perfect image of the moon. He repeated the same story of Ki every class, over and over again. At first, I wondered if this was the only story about Ki he knew, or if he was even aware that he was repeating himself. Then suddenly one day I heard the story as if for the first time and a new understanding emerged—something that cannot be fully articulated. As Pearson would say in class, those who practise Ki cannot positively say *what* Ki is, only *that* Ki is. Dictionaries define the word in many ways (care, concern; intention, inclination; ambience, atmosphere; mood, temper, disposition; and, perhaps most comprehensively, "one's senses," "consciousness," "spirit," "mind," "heart"). These are also strong qualities within story.

If we accept Ki as a form of energy then we can apply the first law of thermodynamics, which states that energy cannot be created or destroyed, only converted from one form to another. My additional teacher of Ki, Robyn Hunt, would also suggest that Ki

> might be thought of as our vital energy, something we experience when we "come into full coordination," as the Alexander Technique masters say, and something—like our breath— which is part of daily life, but which, unless our training specifically awakens us to its presence, often escapes our conscious awareness. We might say it is a way of being in the world, a core idea about our essential energy.[4]

I would add here that this idea also ties us back to our relationship with story, the energy of story, which cannot be created or destroyed, only converted from one form to another.

---

[4] Hunt, Robyn. Personal communication with author. 6 May 2022. This exchange came out of a larger conversation about the role of Ki in training for performance.

If we think of this in the context of performers and audience, then we can explore the exchange of energy as something flowing between the two. The actor extends energy to the audience, and the audience receives it. It is then sent back to the actor, refreshed by the experience of each individual audience member in the house. It becomes a circular exchange that continues through the length of the performance. Some days, this process is more efficient than others, and there can be any number of blocks that impede it. Some members of the audience may be closed off, distracted by something that happened in the day; or the actors may be "phoning in" the performance; or else the ensemble may not have achieved harmony in their rehearsal process. It could be anything. As we are organic creatures, so too is Ki organic, and some days we might be at odds with it. In a very broad simile, one might suggest that it is like living with a spouse or significant other: we need this partner to complete us in life, and we love them very much, but sometimes we are repelled by their very existence and shut ourselves off to them. But when things are in balance and we are all present in the event, we leave the theatre feeling rejuvenated and invigorated, and this could be explained through the notion that we have all just fully exchanged our vital energy for new energy—a complete transfusion. We feel younger, healthy, and inspired to take up dance lessons.

As I emerged out of training and into the profession of theatre, we went right into the formation of the Old Trouts, and so I had to begin to make sense of all this in the context of puppetry. It was some time before I began to tie this extension of Ki between performers and audience to a relationship with the puppet. But I believe that this is what happens: in performance, the puppeteer extends their Ki to the audience, but because their focus is on the puppet, it travels through the puppet to the audience, who are also focused on the puppet, and their own Ki travels the same path back through the puppet to the puppeteer.

Then . . . hop, hop, little frog.

There are many more technical components to the puppeteer's craft that are also important factors to this all working, but to me this energy exchange is a possible last step to making the thing live, and during performance this block of wood is actually imbued with vital energy. We are amazed that it looks so alive because it actually is alive, or at least it is vibrating with living energy. There is also something to this in the collaboration of storytelling.

Stories circulate throughout our lives at a constant rate, and we are often oblivious to their impacts. Kind of like the staggering number of times you touch your face through the day without knowing it: a good pandemic will quickly remind you of those stats. Every day we Make Story, through countless exchanges with people in all walks of life, for a host of different reasons, and not all of the stories we extend are ours. In fact, most of the stories we define ourselves through belong to someone else. We share stories and pass them around like trading cards. Taking bits from other tales and adding them to ours, slowly shifting the deck of things. We adopt these different ways in the telling of stories, gestures we inherit because they delight us, relate to us, or offer a sense of expression that allows us to reach others with greater emotion. They make us the person that we want to become. At least, I for one am willing to admit this in myself.

Not all stories are happy, and sometimes the unhappy ones are those most important to listen to. I find myself driven to change the channel of CBC Radio One when some journalist is taking the story beyond the comfort of my commute, to places where living is hard, even unimaginably so. I reach to change the dial, then remind myself that it is important to invest myself in the story even though it requires stamina to embrace the disharmony in the world. Because hearing the story is important: it is important to receive it to help validate its reality, to acknowledge its reality, and to be better equipped to help in whatever way might be possible. When and if that time comes. Not to suggest that we can do anything in the immediate moment about the stories we hear from the world afar. Many of us are already consumed by the myriad tasks immediately related to our own daily story, just getting home and getting dinner on the table. It can be confounding to the empathetic person who wants to do something to help but can't, for whatever reason; it is debilitating to feel distanced from those stories that we would like to engage with. It is important to hold balance in these situations. We should neither let ourselves off the hook nor move too precipitously to try to help when to offer immediate help is impossible. We are all bound to move in response to wrongs that we feel need to be righted. But how? Sometimes that means being present to simply hear a story, and to receive it, as something to start with, to bear witness.

Hearing the story is the first act. Then we have to make sense of the story: we need to live with it, and to sort through our relationship to it, and to understand our place in it, and its place in the world. This is a much more complex task than it would seem, for very few stories are just as they are. This presents a confounding paradox. Some stories are clear. There need be no debate. I crashed into your car; sorry, I was texting; my insurance will pay. Many more are not clear, in that a single story can be viewed in a multitude of different ways, with each way being truth personified for each different person. This understanding can be exploited by some individuals, and even whole cultures, who are bent on driving their personal agendas over the way of others. Historically, stories have been used to control large bodies of the population: they've been propagated and manipulated to express racist views, to start wars, to perpetrate genocide. It is easy to illustrate how this manipulative process is possible.

He looks to the bottle of water on
stage beside him.

Someone placed this bottle of water here. This is an act of benevolence and kindness. There is concern in this story, as someone has foretold my need to drink water. That I might become fatigued and my throat might get dry. There is another possible story here, though. This bottle could represent the story of how we are unable to move past our disposable habits. That we are so concerned with the forward motion of our lives that we can't be bothered to slow down and manage the simple task of washing reusable receptacles for the sake of a simple drink of water. Then I emerge onstage with my trusty water bottle and shift the story further. A tale now of a noble soul who cares for the environment and who contemplates this disposable plastic bottle with alarm and disgust, and who has taken conscientious steps forward to do their part to combat climate crises. And yet I stand before you with a great carbon footprint, having boarded a jet that carried me more miles than any person should travel in six hours to indulge my vanity by speaking about my reusable water bottle in front of the lovely people of St. John's at the LSPU Hall. In a further sign of presumption, I've arrived in a community of storytellers, to speak to them about the nature of storytelling.

He drinks from his bottle.

It's actually gin in this bottle. And they were going to put a reusable water jug out here, but I told them it didn't serve my purpose.

It's hard—daunting actually—to sort through the mire of those stories that we connect with, to make sense of the world. To understand ourselves. It's important not to surrender to our inner cynics. Even when I prattle on about the failings of humankind, I find a bedrock of optimism under it all. Optimism that the world is inhabited by good people, and at the end of the day the human race is not driven by hidden agendas. Look to stories of natural disaster and we see this. Any flood or earthquake will immediately demonstrate how the collective whole rallies around an ennobling story of human solidarity, offering help and extending compassion. Perhaps this is tied to the reality that most stories are offered with energy that is exchanged from a place of truth and sharing. When it lands without an agenda of personal gain and instead expresses our need to participate in life.

I spoke earlier of my good fortune to be part of a story called *Iniskim: Return of the Buffalo.* "Iniskim" is a Blackfoot word that relates to the buffalo and in particular to a sacred stone, believed to be the buffalo stone, that can be discovered near rivers in southern Alberta. This stone and this word "Iniskim" are also parts of a story about how the buffalo were hidden in a mountain by Napi, the Blackfoot

Trickster. He knew he had to do this to protect them from a great harm that was to befall them. Elders within many First Nation communities share stories about how the buffalo would one day return. And it is happening now. There are initiatives within areas of the US that have started to explore returning the bison to the natural ecosystems there. In 2017, with the creation of the Buffalo Treaty, as well as movement within Environment Canada and various NGOs, bison were reintegrated into the natural landscape of Banff National Park in Alberta—a first step.

According to Ronald Trahan of the Confederated Salish and Kootenai Tribal Council,

> [the] Buffalo Treaty is the first among US Tribes and Canadian First Nations in more than 150 years ... [Over] 40 Tribes and First Nations are working together as treaty signers and have gathered each year to advance its objectives. The goal of the Buffalo Treaty Celebration is to combine our voices to achieve the ecological restoration of the buffalo that have been at the heart of our cultural traditions for thousands of years.[5]

5   Trahan, Ronald. "Buffalo Treaty." *Iniskim: Return of the Buffalo*. August 2022. Program.

This is community coming together not to create story but to add to story, to join in story. The buffalo have been around longer than any account can hold. Science might suggest a possible length of time, but that would entail a linear temporal understanding. As I was guided through the artistic process of *Iniskim* by Indigenous Elders, I found myself discovering a more circular relationship to things. At once I was reunited with the repetitive lecturing of my aikido sensei by the Indigenous view of time. Dr. Leroy Little Bear, a scholar of the Blackfoot Confederacy and member of the Kainai Nation in southern Alberta, describes it like this:

> Blackfoot notions of time (probably more correct to say space) conceal a metaphysics that is very different from Western notions of time. Western notions of time are: linear, forever unfolding in a uniform sense from a point and into the future. It is about past, present, and future, with humans breaking that endless flow into manageable units such as seconds, minutes, hours, days, weeks, months, years . . . Blackfoot think about time from a repetitive perspective. For instance, it is the same day repeated itself. Tomorrow is not a new day. It

will be the same day repeating itself.
Time is an unfolding of a phasing in a
place from subjective reality into
objective and back into subjective.

He goes on to explain that

[there] is a cosmic phasing and a local
phasing. The local phasing is somewhat
similar to Western notions but not the
same. Similar in the sense that in
Blackfoot one can go from the present
and move forward into tomorrow, and
the day after tomorrow. In like manner
one can go backwards from the "now"
to yesterday, and to the day before
yesterday. Blackfoot stop after the two-
day forward or backward. The only
physical reality is the "now." Past and
future are subjective. Everything beyond
the two-day realm amalgamates the
Western notions of past, present, and
future into "just is." [6]

Time was, I found myself invited into this
story. I was asked by one person to meet
another person who introduced me to yet
another person, and suddenly I was writing
arts grants to various organizations to gather
the funds to realize possibilities that hadn't

[6]   Little Bear, Leroy. "Blackfoot Notions of Local Phasing."
      Iniskim: Return of the Buffalo. August 2022. Program.

even been figured yet. Here again, Dr. Little Bear's words on time ring true within my body, as I find myself experiencing the endless repetition of arts granting. And yet as I drafted these funding applications, I sensed something new and different, something lifting my efforts. It was a unique sensation, one I had never felt before. It was as though I was a medium being guided by some unknown force, and the grant was writing itself. I began to understand that this project was being requested by the spirit of the Buffalo themselves, that it was something they wanted done and we were the agents being gathered to the task.

As the cohort formed that would become the core of creators determining how this story would be told, we found ourselves being guided by Elders of the Blackfoot and Stoney Nakoda First Nations. These Knowledge Keepers offered stories and insights that were connected to older ways of knowing and that allowed us to access an artistic process informed by the land. To anchor this idea of creating land-based art, the entire group of artists sequestered itself in an artistic retreat that was hosted at Camp Chief Hector, the summer camp where the Old Trout Puppet Workshop met many years prior, according to linear time. But if you think of it in terms of the Blackfoot ways of knowing, the Old Trouts had been there in an abstract heretofore that might as well have been only two days ago. Things began to make more sense in regard to this place and how it is connected to my sense of story.

In that not-so-distant past, when we rampaged through life as camp counsellors, when we ran amok with the imagination of the kids in our care, filling our days with endless adventure and fun, when we discovered a comradery among kindred spirits and formed fast artistic friendships that would last beyond the life of most rock bands, I'd had a small moment of clarity. I paused in all of it to make sense of why this time in life was such a gift: how could this be so exact and yet so random? It couldn't be coincidence.

The camp was formed in 1926 by YMCA Calgary and has been in operation ever since. It is located in the Bow Valley corridor, just west of the Morley Reserve, which is the home of the Stoney Nakoda First Nations. The Stoneys are actually Sioux, and they had been in the Bow Valley for hundreds of years, having migrated west from the area of the Lakota Sioux sometime in the 1600s. At least, that is the history as paraphrased in the colonial archives of Calgary's Glenbow Museum. To fully understand things, you would have to sit and listen to the story of the Stoney Elders. Here they'd lived in concert with the land, finding the truest understanding of themselves within and through the land, as part of the land, not simply living on it and taking from it. Their energy infused the land, and somehow we were being energized by it. This is the possibility that had opened up to me, fuelled by my study of, and investment in, the idea of Ki. This energy was finding its way into us, to be shared by us, and the result was expressing itself in creative ways; it was manifesting itself as new story.

Again stepping away from the conveniences of modern living, we again placed ourselves in what might seem a simpler way of being but in fact makes things physically more complicated. We had to carry our water to our studio space, we had to light fires to stay warm in the cool air of mountain mornings, we had to hike fair distances to gather the necessities for our artistic process. We needed each other and we cared for each other through that need. In some manner, we placed hardship in the path of our artistic process. And in so doing we found ourselves guided once more by the spirit of the buffalo. The buffalo is the only animal who stands to face the oncoming storm. All other animals flee the onslaught and seek shelter from it. The buffalo confronts it head on.

As we worked in this way and dug in to discover the arc of our story, I experienced a conflict on an existential level. I found myself asking how I fit into this story. The connection of the Indigenous artists and storytellers to the spirit of the buffalo was immense. I found myself asking an important question: am I just a servant to someone else's story, or do I have a place in it as well? Does the fabric of this story help to make me who I am? Or am I a tourist in this tale, hijacking its importance to fulfill my own vanity? Is there authenticity in me helping to tell this? I grappled with this question for some time. When I put this question to Amethyst First Rider, who's now the Artistic Director of the project, she explained it like this, and I paraphrase: stories are only energy; they exist as energy. She suggested that in this way no one person can own a story, stories can only be shared between people. When you engage in storytelling, or story-listening, you engage in a collective activity and everyone has a place of participation in it. As you participate you join the energy of the story, in some manner become part of the story. If all we are is story, then the importance of how we engage in and with story becomes paramount.

Can you remember the first story that you ever told? Can you remember the last story you told? Maybe you just told one, sitting here, waiting for this. Can you remember the details? Why did you tell that story? What did you hope to gain from the telling? Was it a true story, or a not-true story? Most are both, I wager. There are various ways to tell if someone is lying to you:

> People tend to change their head position quickly.
>
> Their breathing may also change.
>
> They tend to stand very still and may repeat words or phrases . . . words or . . . phrases.
>
> They may provide too much information. (*He thinks for a moment.*) On my flight here I didn't have time to eat and couldn't bring myself to buy the stale sandwich on the plane (*pause*); the guy sitting next to me ordered the lasagna and some red wine and breathed heavily through his nose (*pause*); I really wished I had got that lasagna.
>
> They may cover or touch their mouth. (*He thinks for a moment.*) But as we've

been told by various health organizations, we touch our face up to twenty-three times an hour, so this might not be the best indicator.

And often, they spout about how they can make a nation great again; this one is generally easy to spot, but you'd be surprised.

Most of us are in a constant state of reckoning with our stories—again, sorting through the mire of those stories that we connect to, to make sense of the world. In this reckoning is a desire to discover truth in ourselves and to make sense of this truth in respect to the effort that life takes. To make sense of a life lived. Here also we enter into the double edge of stories, and that of truth. When we work in mask, particularly full character mask, we're encouraged to explore something that the great French theatre artist Jacques Lecoq referred to as the "contramask," or counter mask. This is that invisible opposite to the literal expression we see on the character mask. If we think we are working with a "happy" character then we should seek to discover the opposite nature of this person. Until you have embraced the contramask, you haven't fully plumbed the complete person.

Often truth carries a contramask. This is the kind of thing that demagogues exploit when riling the crowds at their rallies. They find that other sense of meaning within truth and then posit this as truth verbatim—the only truth. Stories carry truths within them for us to discover, but how do we reconcile ourselves with the contramasks of truth? It is tricky, and there may never be a system that enables this. Often (although not always) there is a motivation behind the telling of a story, and often there is a specific reason to listen to the story. But we are creatures of convenience; we all want things to be simple, make sense, and not require too much effort—or at least this last point seems to be a trend I am noticing in myself and in others as we sink deeper into the luxury of the digital age. And more and more people are reaching toward that digital connection to find the stories that will define them, and it is a terrible irony that they lose themselves in the process.

The reason that there are so many cars on the planet is that their invention was perfect. The design of the car serves the individual in the exact way that it is needed. This is not to speak of the negative impact it has had upon the environment and its contribution to what is called global warming, but this is not the fault of the car. Digital devices are very similar in this respect, a perfect design delivering perfect access to limitless selections of story. The flaw here isn't in the device but in the human propensity to want more, now. More than ever, we have any manner of story at our fingertips, and while we may think these stories are helping to define who we are, through our insatiable need to consume we are flitting from one to the next without immersing ourselves in any—without participating in the story or collaborating to discover a deeper relationship to the truths within that story. To that which we can use to help define our place in the world.

Recently, a prize was awarded to a video game designer at the Colorado State Fair in their Digital Arts competition. First prize, to a piece that was created using "an artificial intelligence program that can turn text descriptions into images."[7] As the story goes, this has sparked a series of responses on the internet from folks who are concerned for the sake of art. As you can imagine, the implications are grim for those who fancy themselves illustrators. What will happen to the craft of art-making? Where do we hold

[7] Kuta, Sarah. "Art Made with Artificial Intelligence Wins at State Fair." *Smithsonian Magazine*, 6 September 2022, https://www.smithsonianmag.com/smart-news/artificial-intelligence-art-wins-colorado-state-fair-180980703/.

the journey of human mastery and working with our hands? How warm can a digital quilt keep you?

In some respect the crafting of our stories is also at stake here. How are we able to develop those kinds of physical relationships in the sharing of our stories that will enable palpable exchanges of energy when we rely on the fast fix delivered by our Android device? How can we connect in ways that drive us to enquire about how we fit into the stories that we gather? How do we elevate our need to find a truth that truly defines and makes us who we are? How do we collaborate so that we are not simply the voyeurs of someone else's journey?

Maybe one day they will begin to regulate this perfect invention, this digital access to all, for the sake of our own health, like when they initiated laws to make us wear seatbelts, an infringement on our personal rights, yet now accepted with not even a second thought. You just wear one. Or maybe we will come to a place in our lives where we discover the empirical need to be connected to human beings, and that a million stories aren't the answer, and as with a good meal you need to slow down and take your time moving through it. That bingeing only leads to bloat and confusion. Perhaps we will realize that stories are actually nutrients required to live and not something just to soothe our boredom or to mask our inability to be at peace with our own emotional journey.

I stand before you less because of anything I alone have done, and more because of the people that I've gathered around me, or those that I've found myself with, and often by the operation of forces unknown to me. An irony in my story is that I graduated from high school with the lowest GPA of anyone in my graduating class. Still, I sat at the head table during the final banquet, next to the Valedictorian, and gave the Class Historian speech. It was funnier than the serious speech that was telling us that we were ready for life. Somehow, I knew everyone that I went to school with, and I had been collecting stories with them.

Now here I am, delivering the Pratt Lecture, a lecture series that has been attended by remarkable people, delivered at the LSPU Hall, a place with a remarkable history of its own. Who could have guessed this journey?

I am here because I do not reach toward a singular story but rather commit myself to others to discover a collective whole to that story that I do not control, adding what I can to a living organism of unpredictable shape. This is to face the storm inherent in not being in control—to collaborate. This is where I am most grateful for your inclusion in the process. Already things have shifted. Not to suggest that I do not exercise directive force toward the outcome—I stamp my feet like the rest of them and reach toward self-serving goals when it suits me or when I can (even those objectives that are for the greater good but also define me as the caring person I want to be). But to collaborate is to release. To release is to widen one's self in the world. To embrace those things that don't immediately make sense, and not to allow frustration into the process of meaning-making, but to sit with a modicum of assurance that at some point, some understanding will land. It's okay to not understand every moment fully, not to be in control of that understanding.

> *He looks as though suddenly remembering the long piece of paper that he dragged out. With some sense of urgency, he begins to quickly fold up the paper and stuff it into his little suitcase. He takes one more quick drink of water.*

Hilarious.

ACKNOWLEDGEMENTS

This lecture is an effort to reach two days back and two days forward from the present moment in which we've all landed. It rests upon the vital energy of many individuals and I am grateful to be included in the process of sharing it.

The script *Iniskim: Return of the Buffalo* was conceived and first performed in 2017 in the Bow Valley Corridor at YMCA Camp Chief Hector. This project has been guided by the knowledge of Blackfoot Elders Raymond Many Bears, Dr. Leroy Little Bear, and Amethyst First Rider, and by Stoney Nakoda Elder Rod Hunter and Elder-in-the-making Anders Hunter. Our cohort includes Nan Balkwill and David Lane. These individuals have stretched my understanding of one's place in the world.

"To Be Honest, We Devised Theatre Companies Are Kind of like Gangs" was first published by *Canadian Theatre Review* and written by Judd Palmer in the early studio days when we all lived together amidst the dust, puppets, mice, and crusts of bread. The article would go on to inform our eighth full-scale puppet show, *Ignorance*, which toured across Canada and on to France, Spain, Denmark, and Romania. Words cannot express my deep dependence on the members of the Old Trout Puppet Workshop: they are buffalo to me.

Notes on the work of Tadashi Suzuki and the presence of Ki in performance grew out of my training with Professors Steve Pearson and Robyn Hunt at the Professional Actor Training Program at the University of Washington from 1997 to 2000. Their unique approach is partly the result of their participation in Mr. Suzuki's theatre company for some twelve years, as well as intensive work with Shogo Ohta between 1994 and 2000, and it continues with their co-direction of the Pacific Performance Project/East (P3/East), which they founded in 1994. The impact of their training methodology has greatly informed my journey in teaching and art-making.

My thanks and appreciation to Andrew Loman, whom I count as an old friend and who was witness to the formative years of those individuals who would become the Old Trouts as we all tromped through Kananaskis Country together making interpretive shows about rocks, wildflowers, and bats—one can never forget the bats. This lecture would not make any sense if it were not for his keen eye and that of Claire Wilkshire, editor at Breakwater Books. For the deft formatting of the manuscript I extend my thanks to Rhonda Molloy.

Peter Balkwill

AUTHOR PHOTO | J U N O **BALKWILL**

PETER **BALKWILL**

Peter Balkwill is a founding co-artistic director at the Old Trout Puppet Workshop in Calgary, Alberta, whose internationally acclaimed productions include *The Unlikely Birth of Istvan*, *Beowulf*, *The Last Supper of Antonin Carême*, *Famous Puppet Death Scenes*, *The Erotic Anguish of Don Juan*, and *Ghost Opera*. Peter is also co-artistic director—curator of live performance for the International Festival of Animated Objects, as well as the founder and educational director of the Canadian Academy of Mask and Puppetry. He is an assistant professor in the School of Creative and Performing Arts at the University of Calgary.

ALSO IN THIS SERIES

The Quest for a "National" Nationalism:
E. J. Pratt's Epic Ambition, "Race" Consciousness,
and the Contradictions of Canadian Identity
George Elliott Clarke

The Vernacular Strain in Newfoundland Poetry
Mary Dalton